Fuck Off

Stress Relief Coloring Book With

Swear World

By

S.B. Nozaz

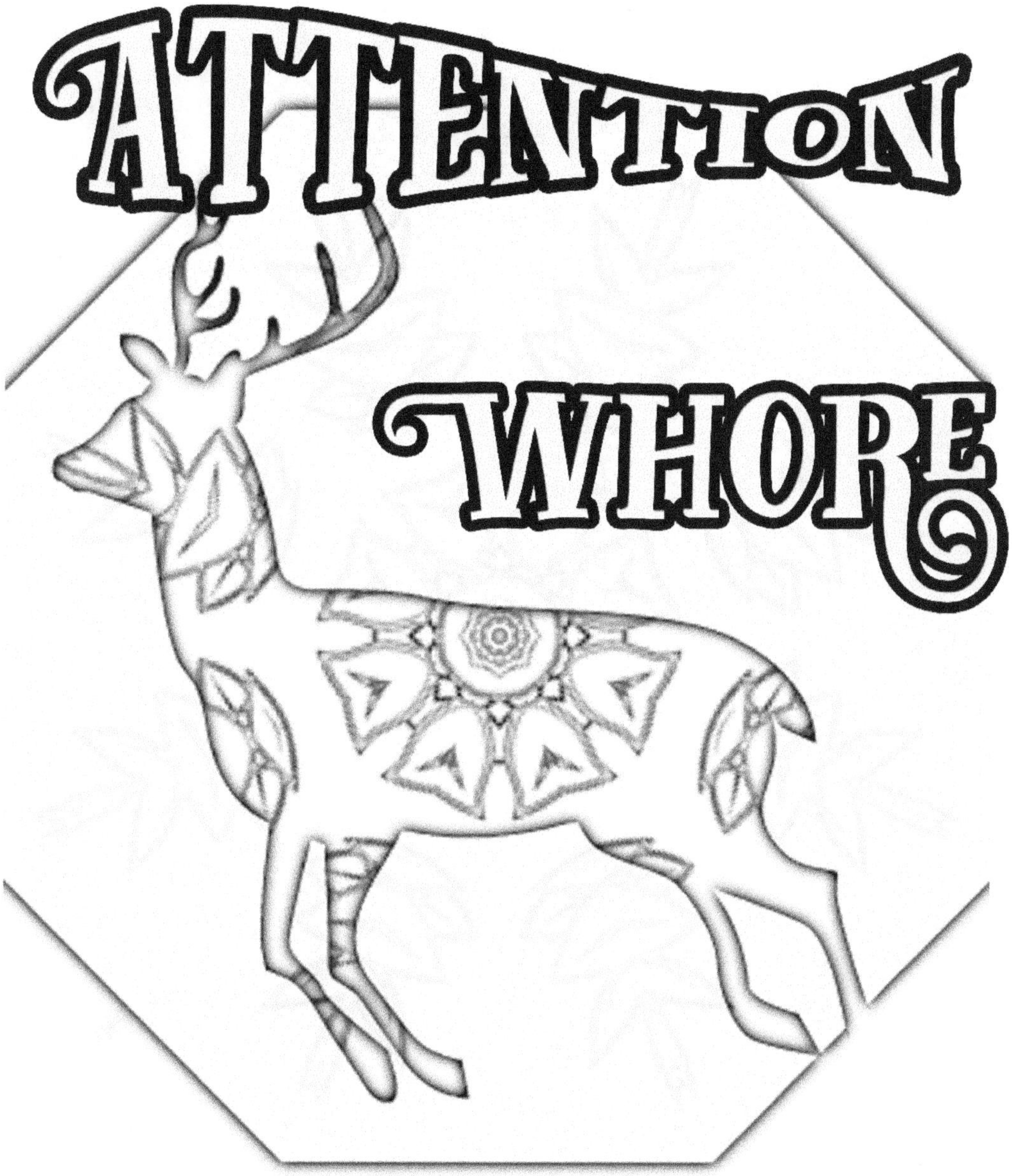
ATTENTION
WHORE

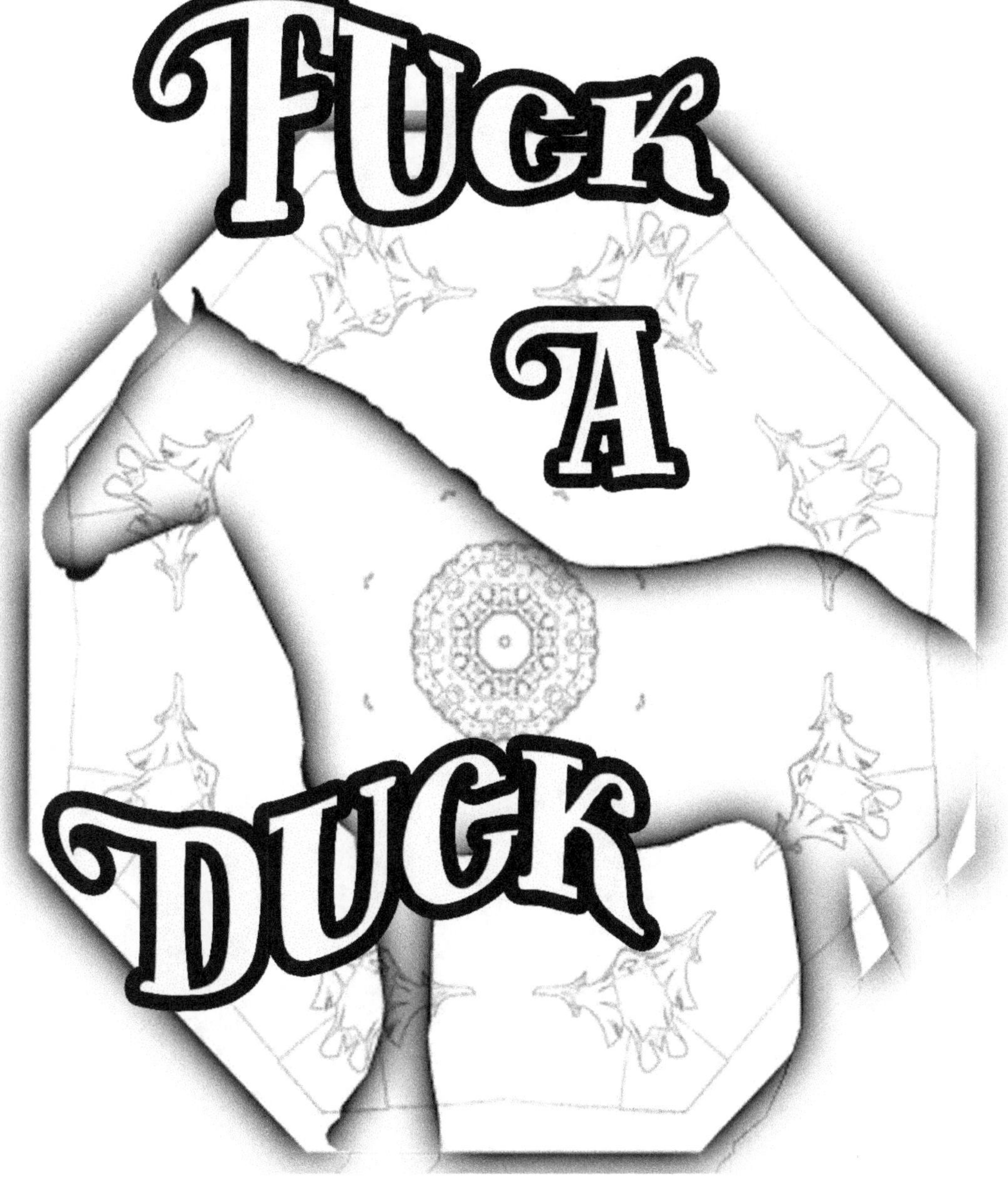
FUCK
A
DUCK

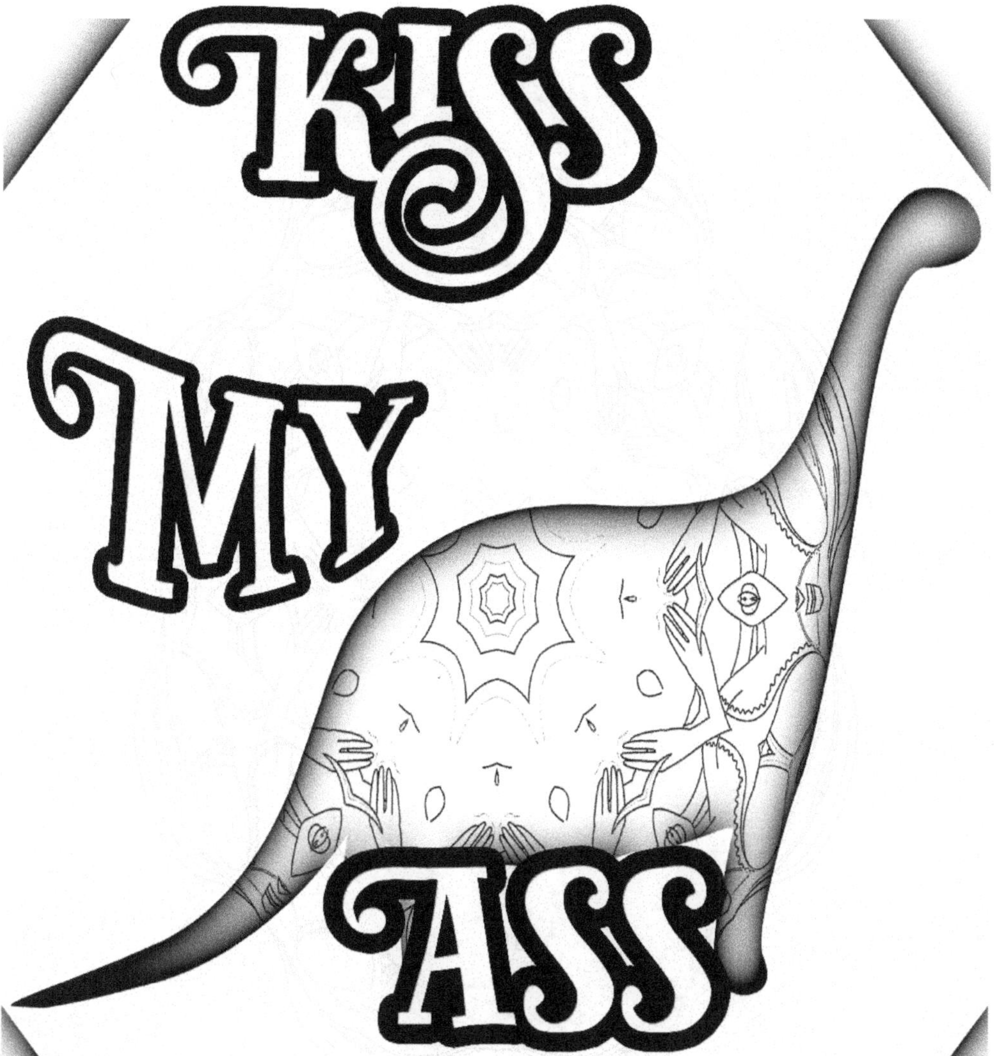
KISS
MY
ASS

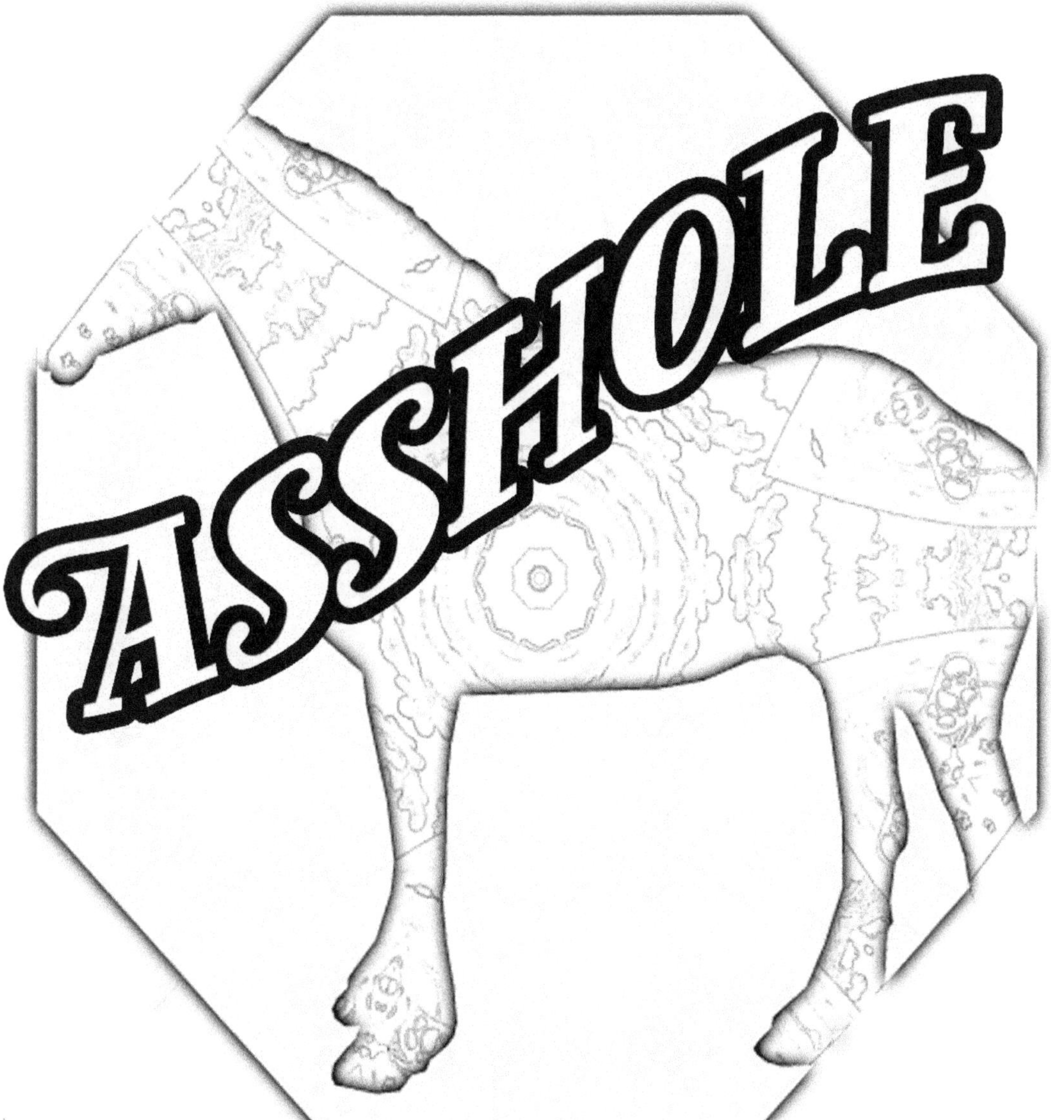
ASSHOLE

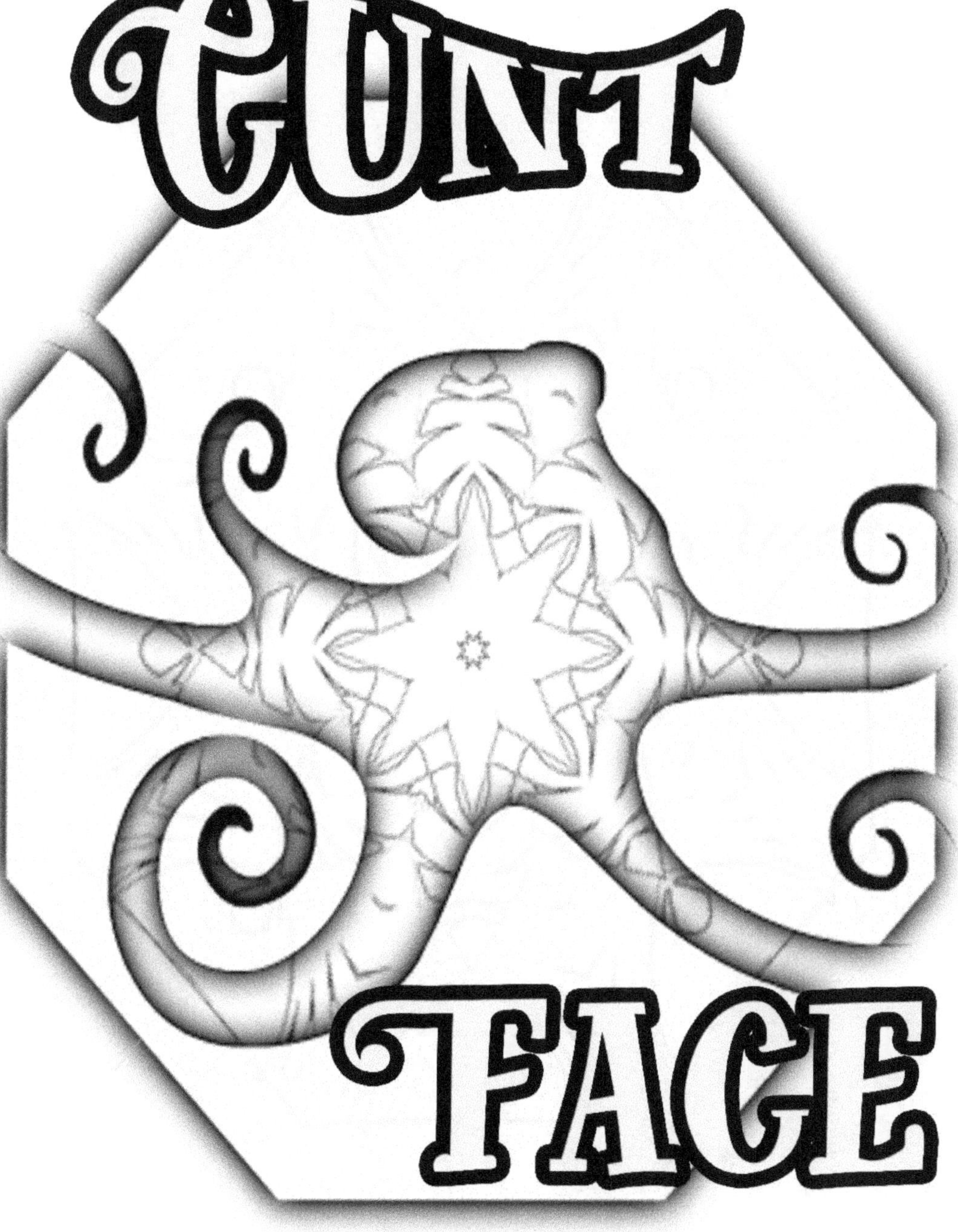
CUNT
FACE

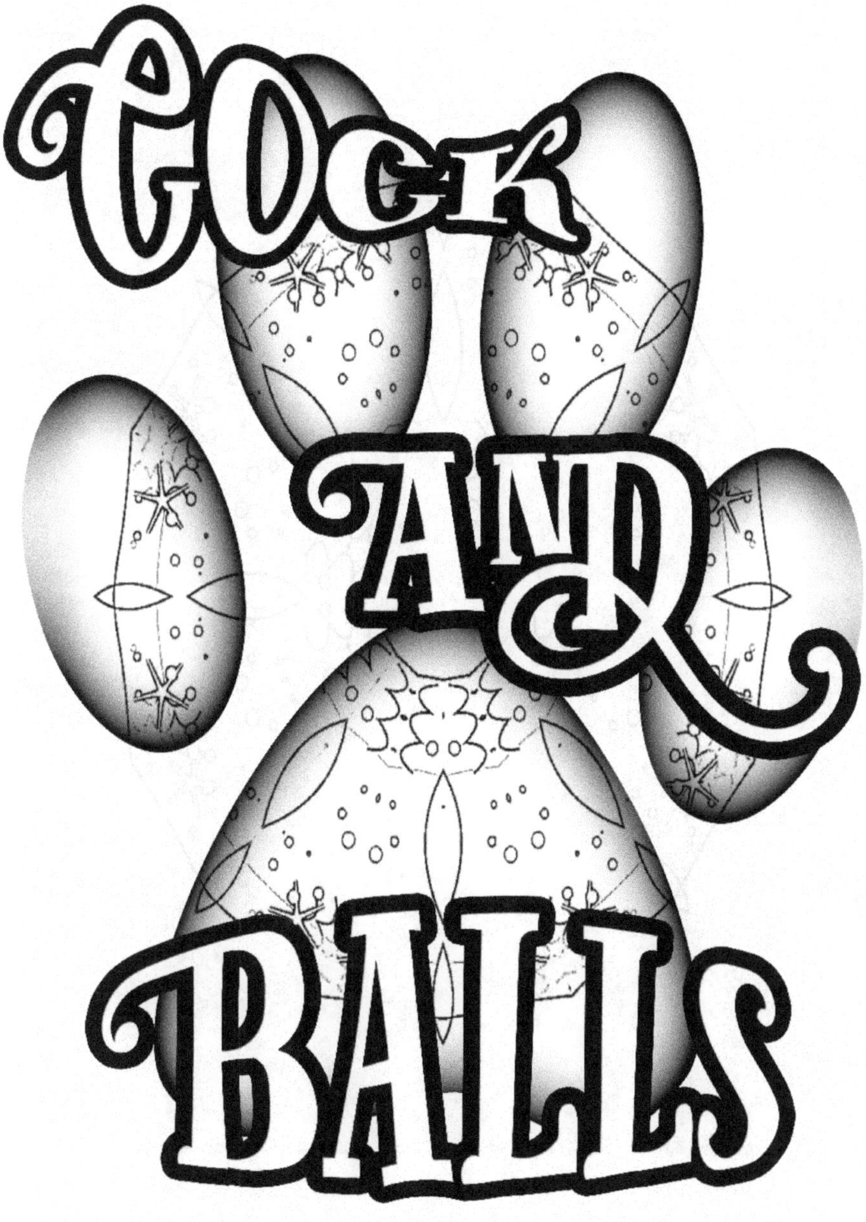
COCK
AND
BALLS

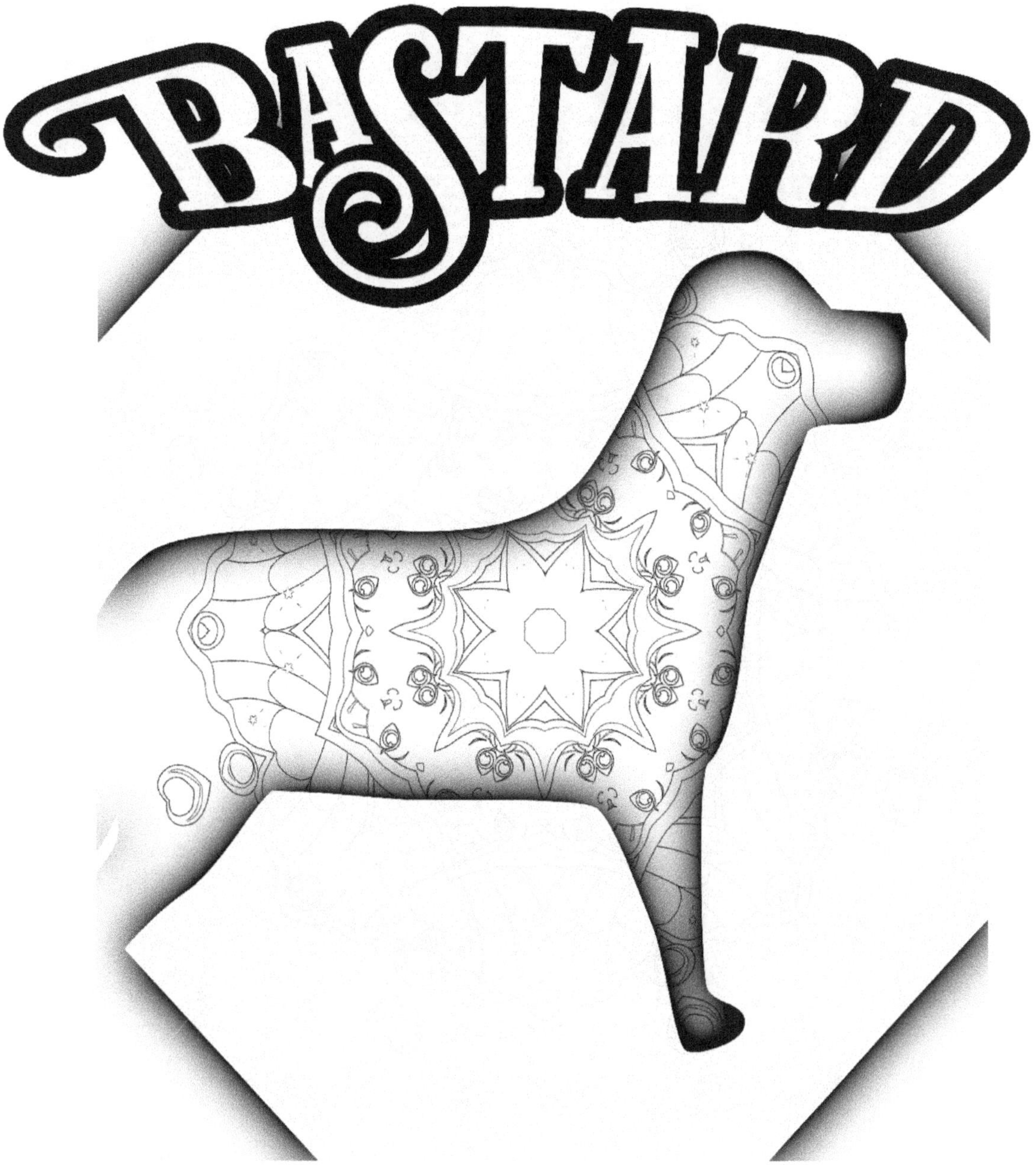
BASTARD

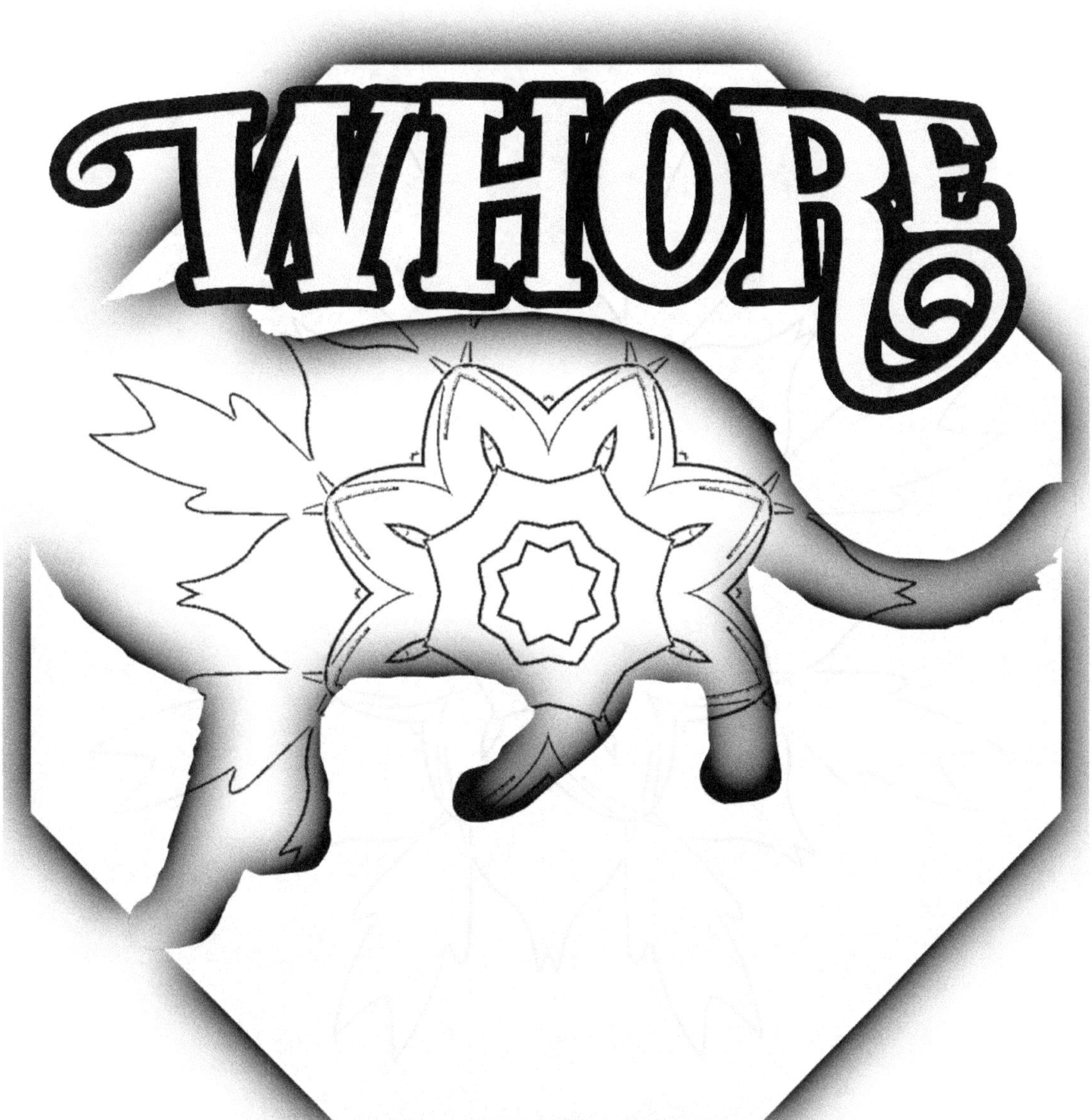
WHORE

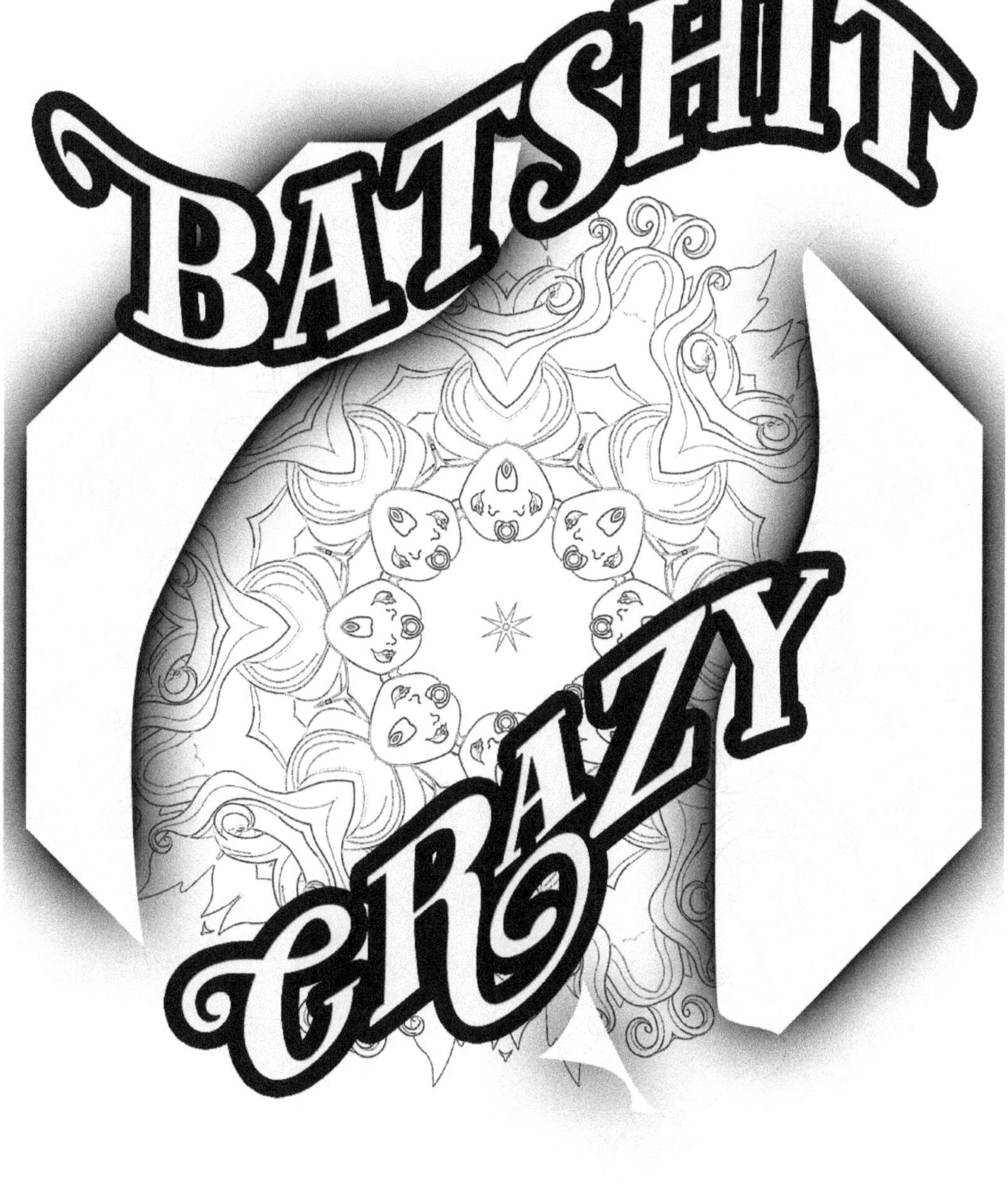
BATSHIT
CRAZY

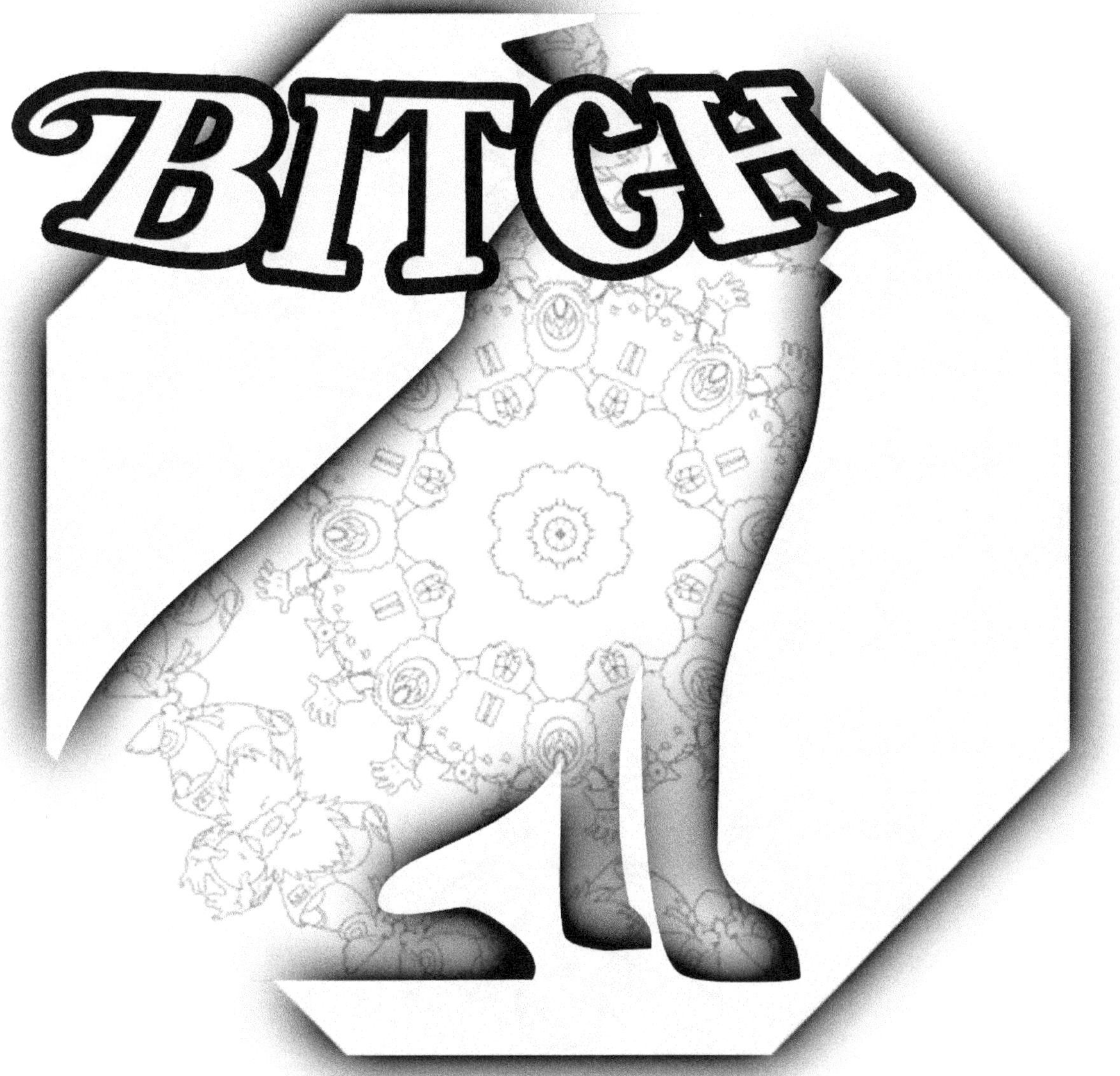
BITCH

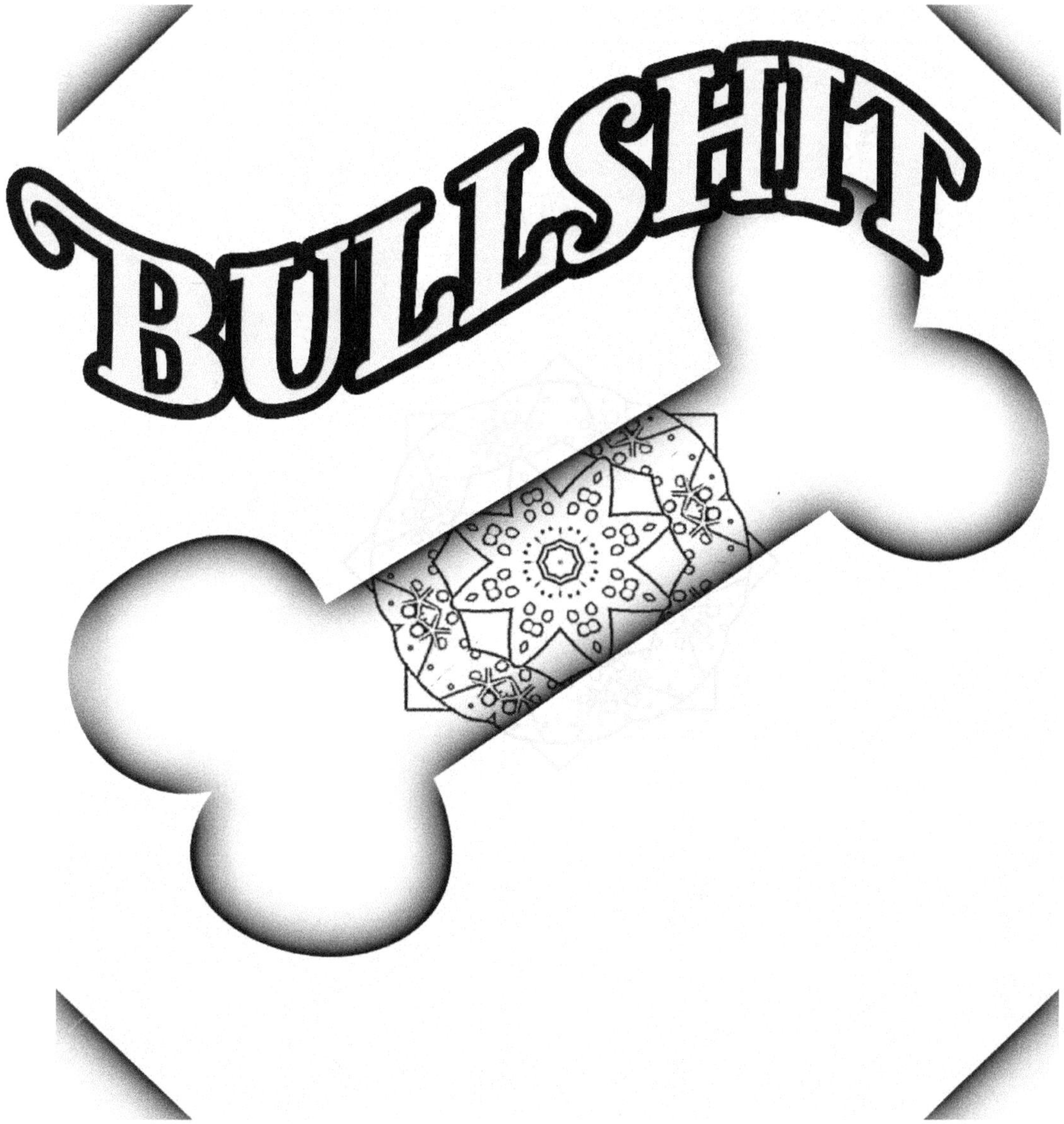
BULLSHIT

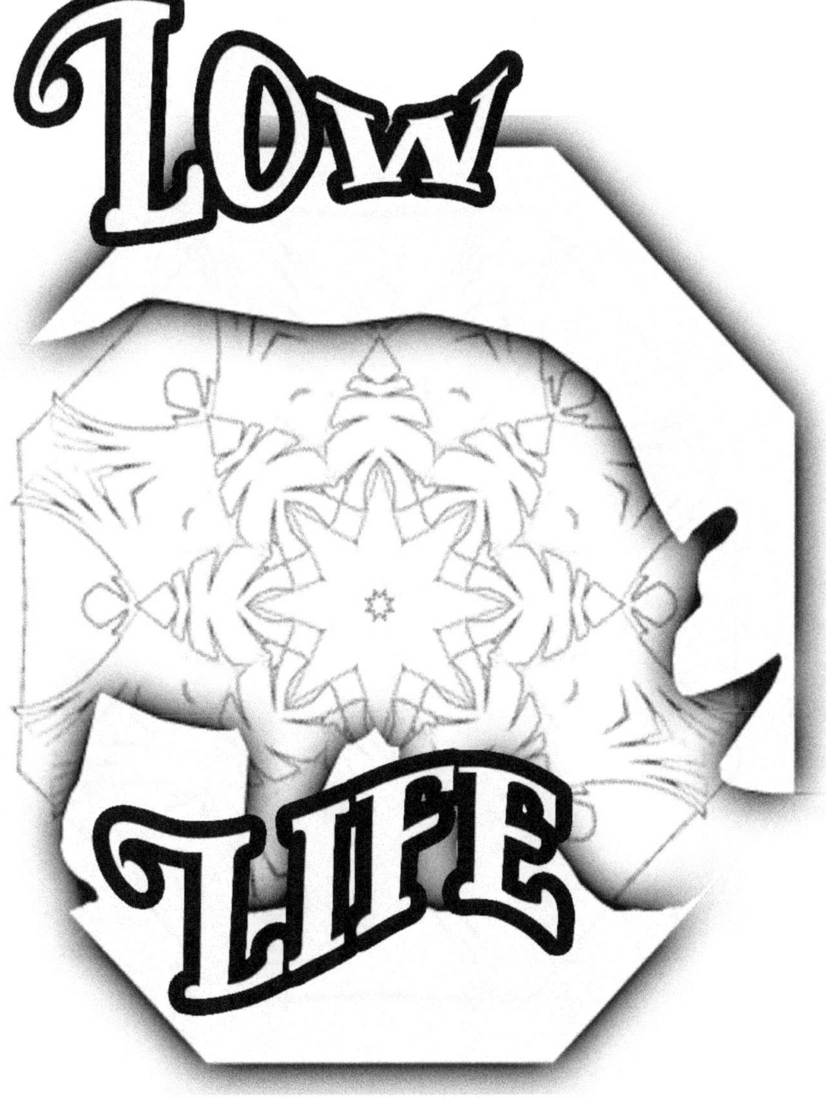
Low
LIFE

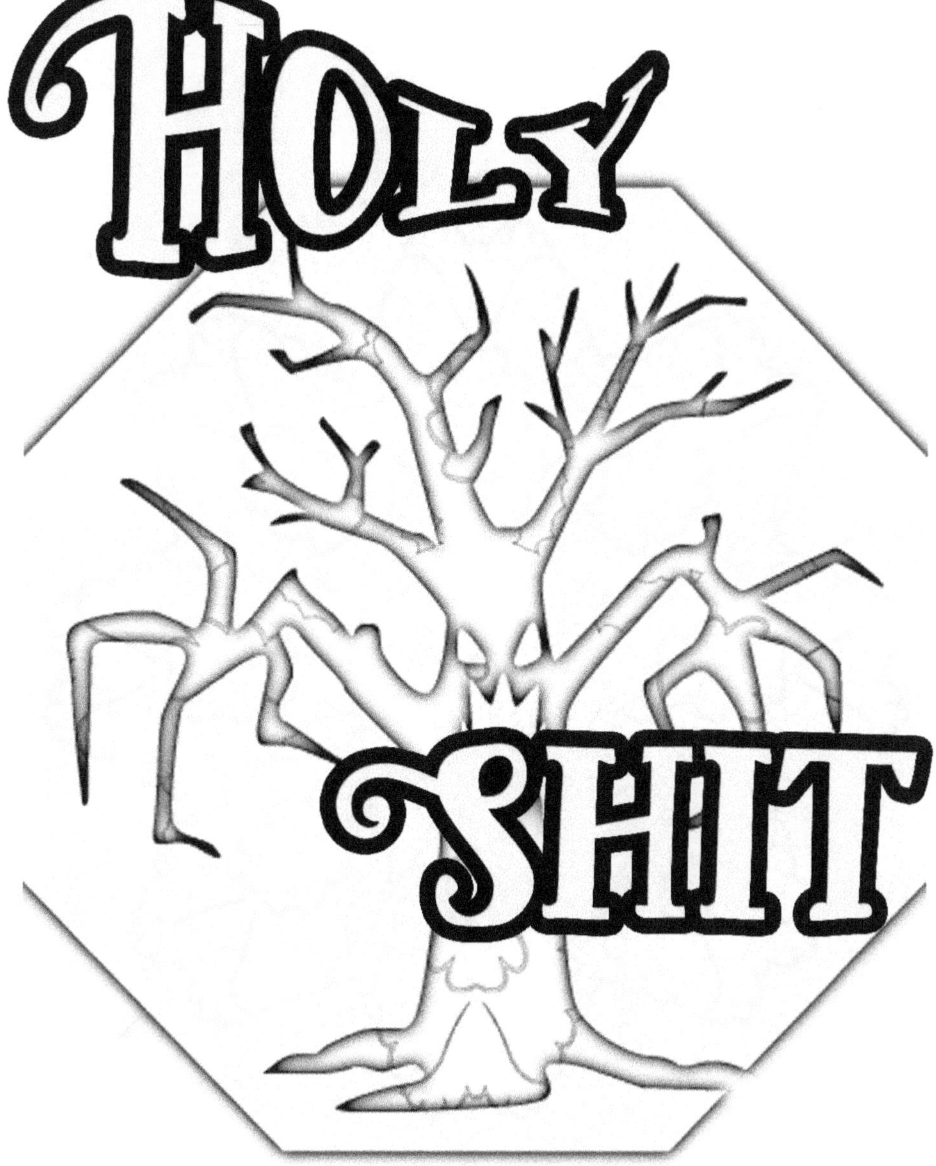
HOLY
SHIT

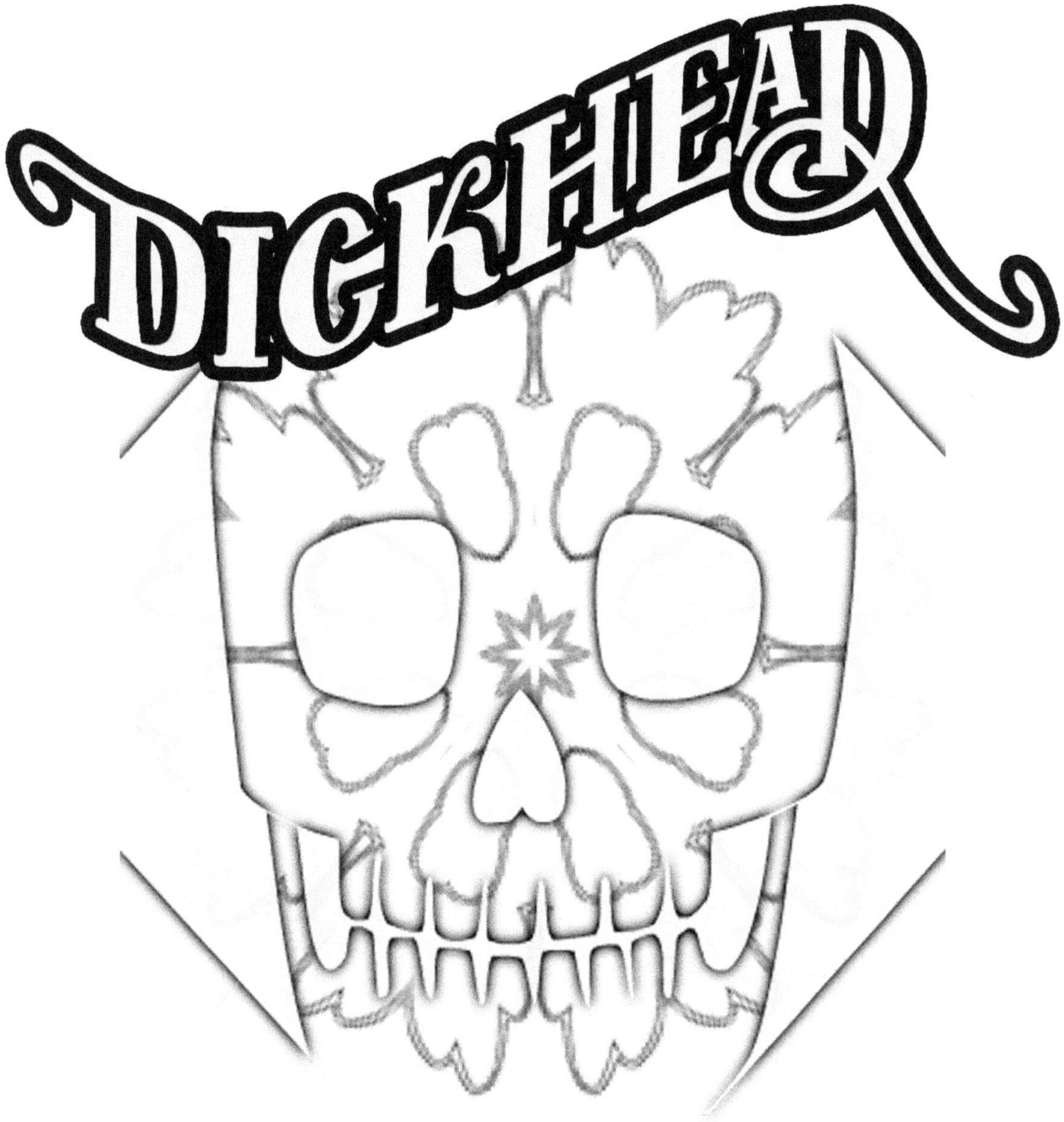
DICKHEAD

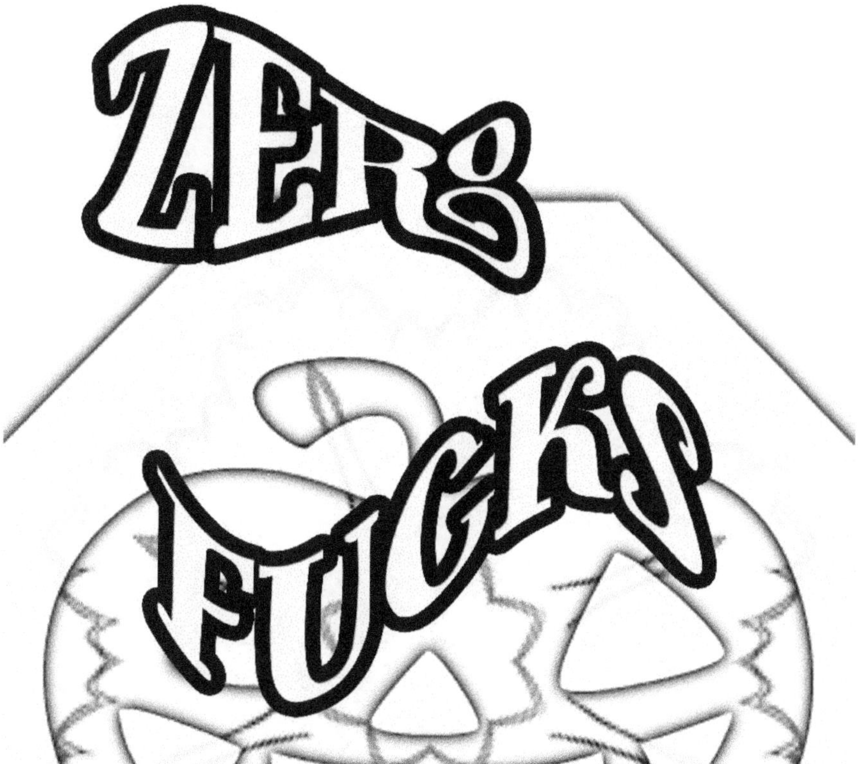
ZERO
FUCKS
GIVEN

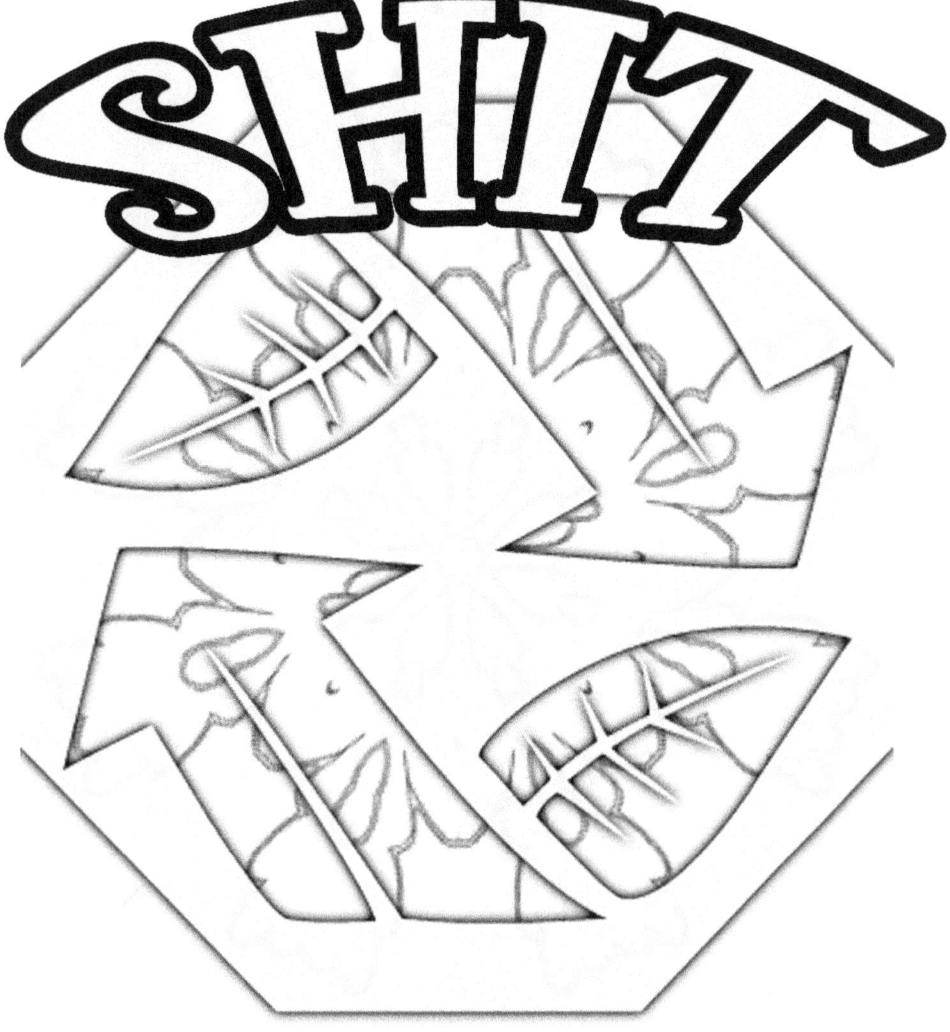
SHIT

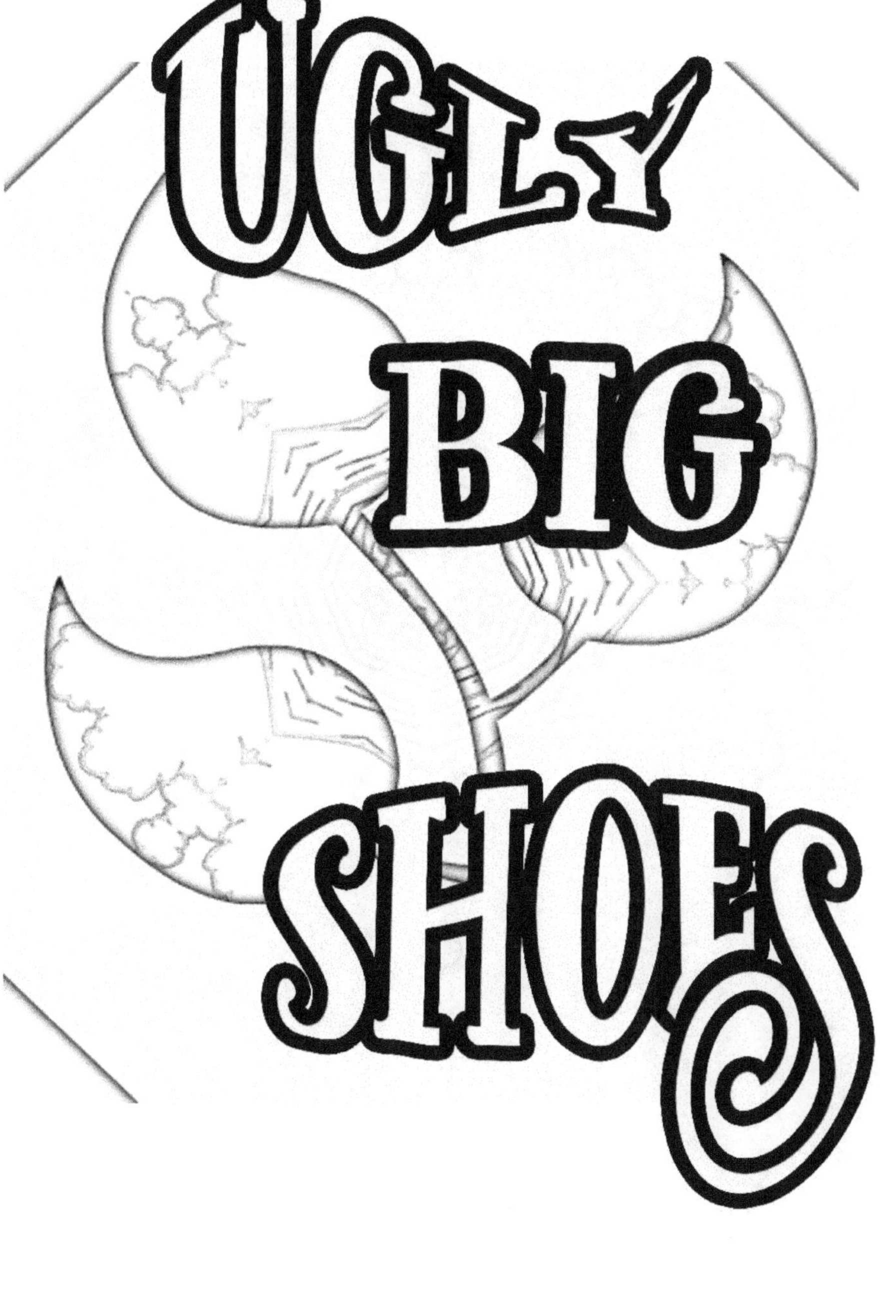
UGLY
BIG
SHOES

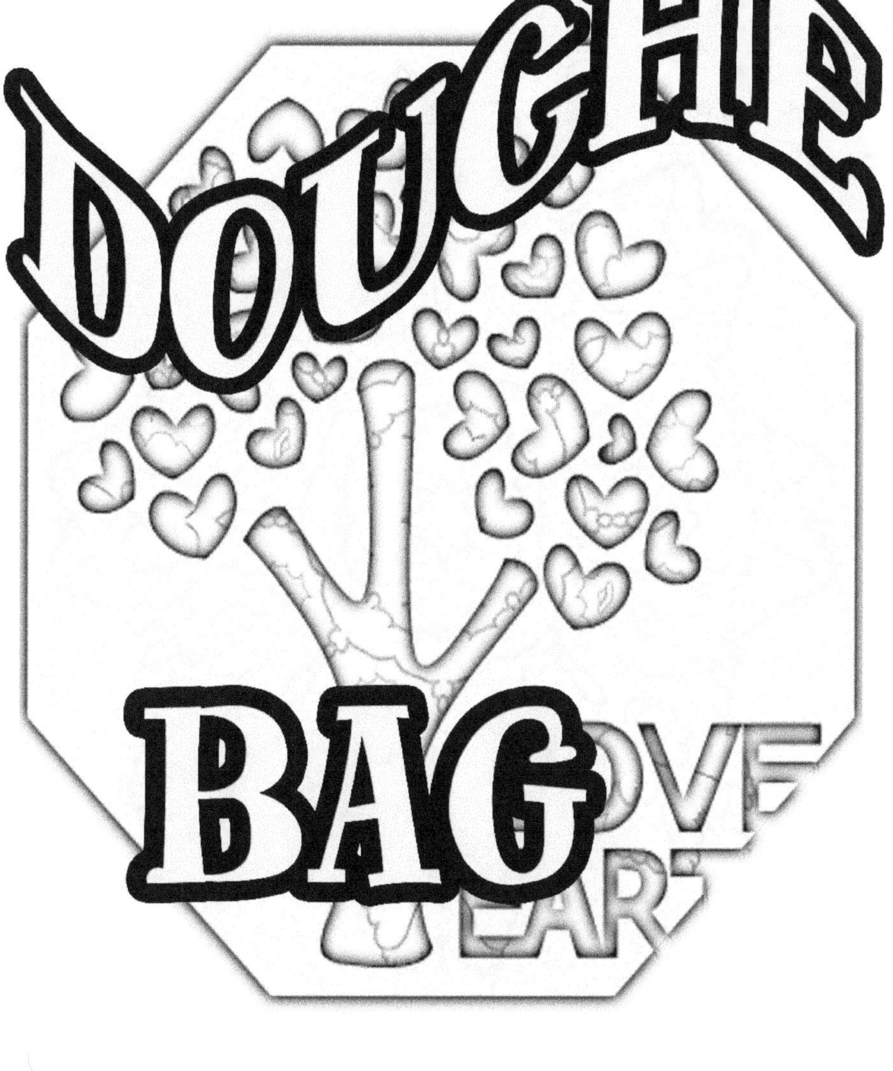
DOUCHE
BAG

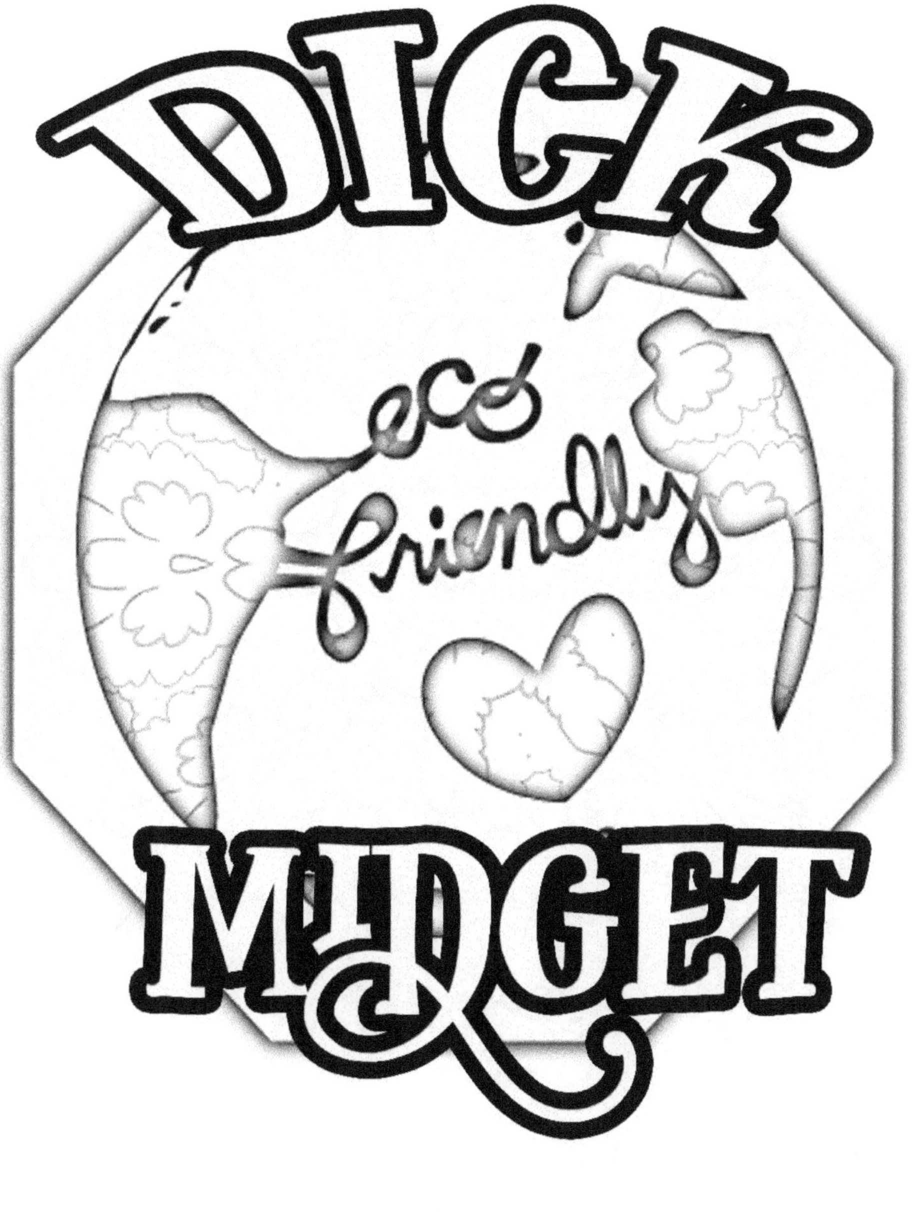
DICK
eco friendly
MIDGET

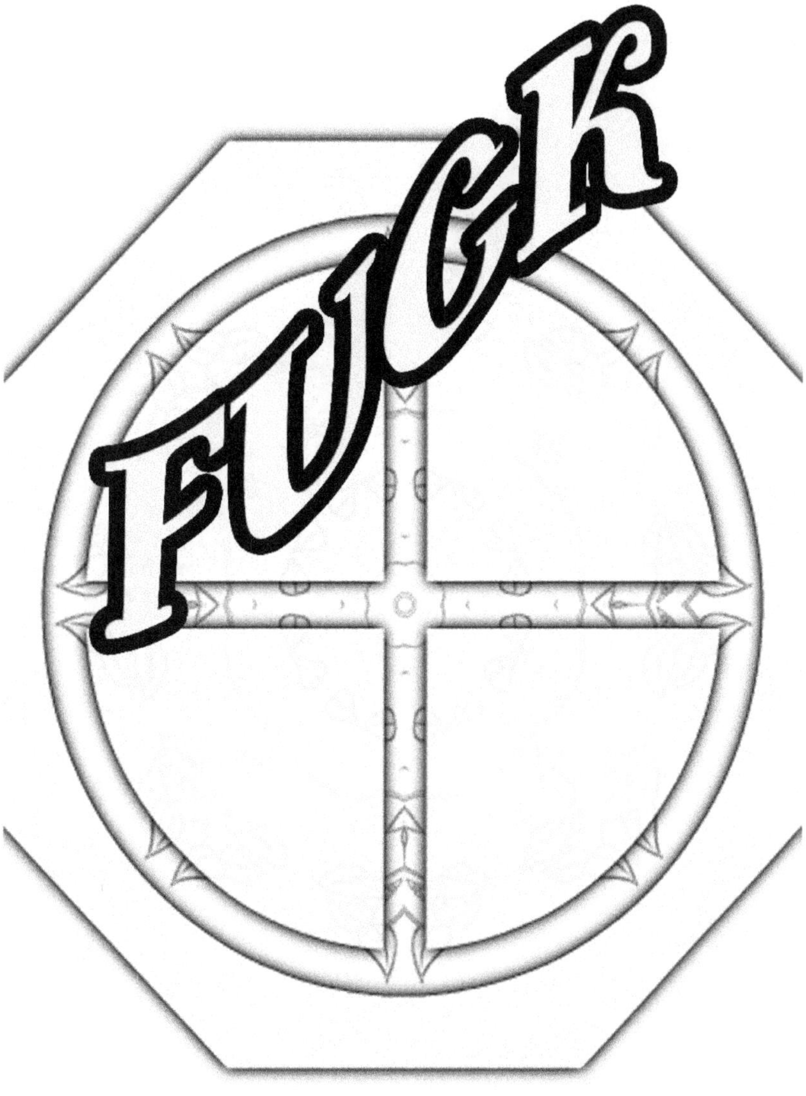
FUCK

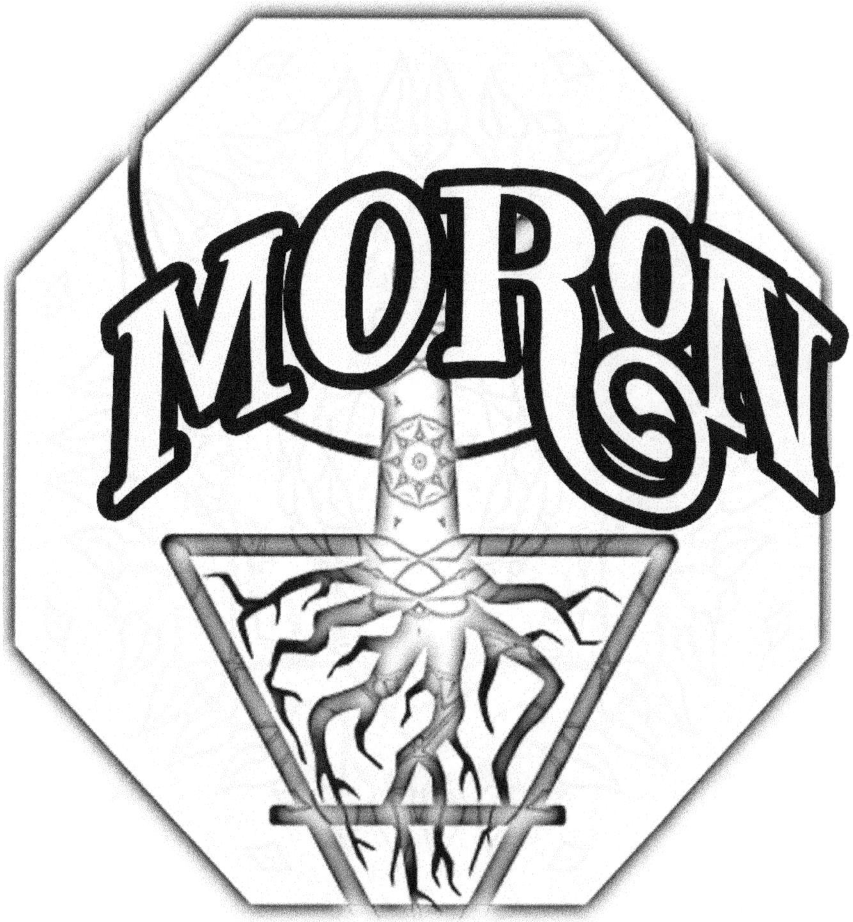
MORON

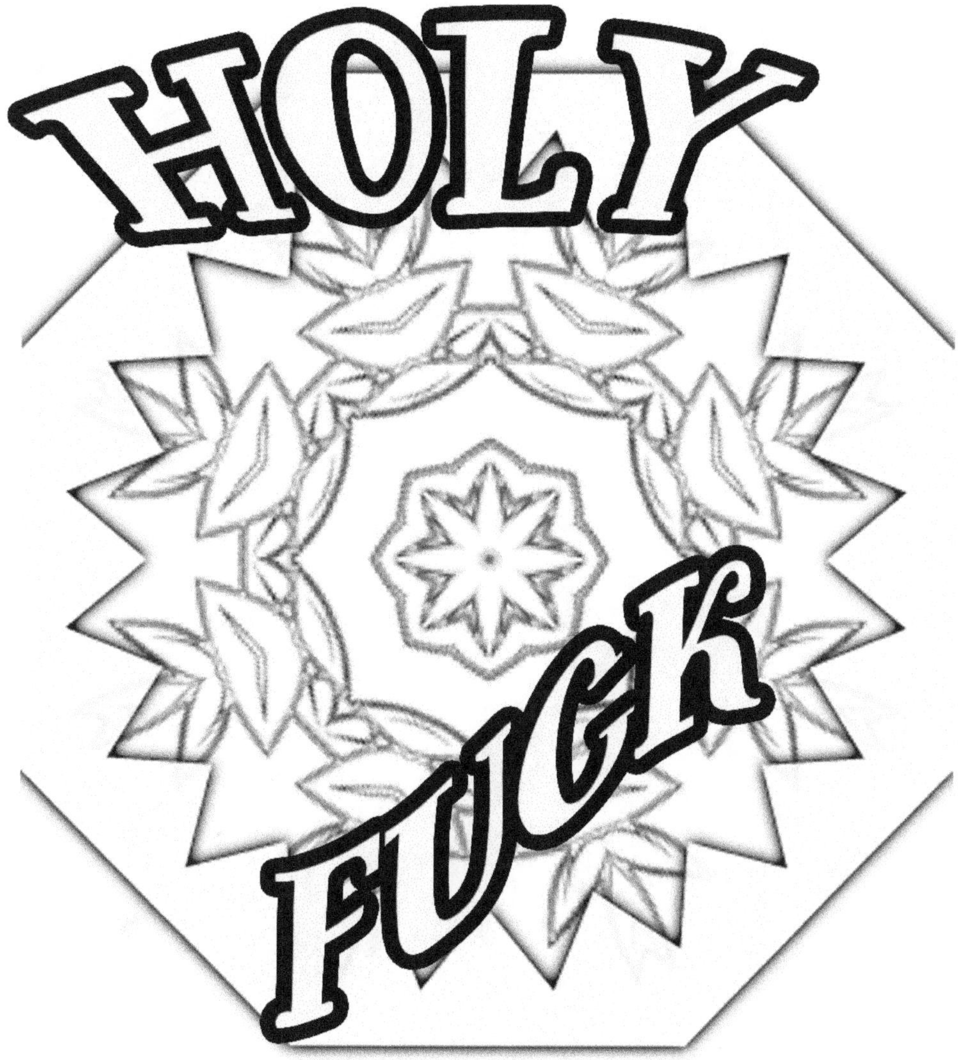
HOLY
FUCK

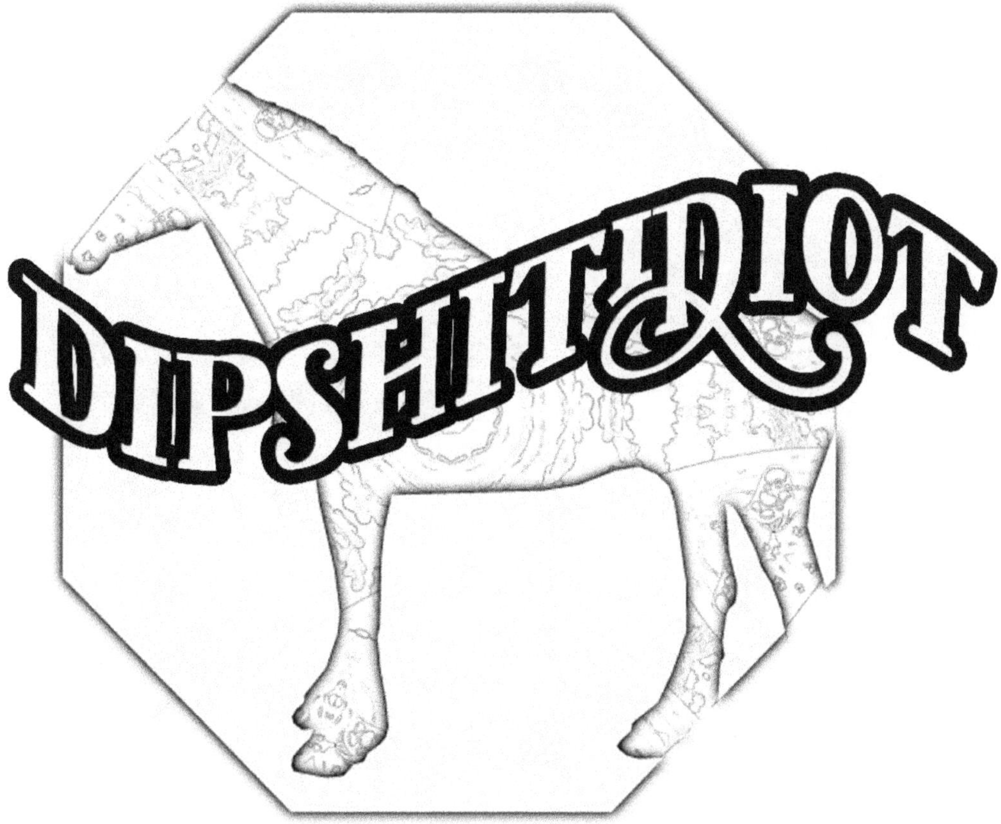
DIPSHITIDIOT

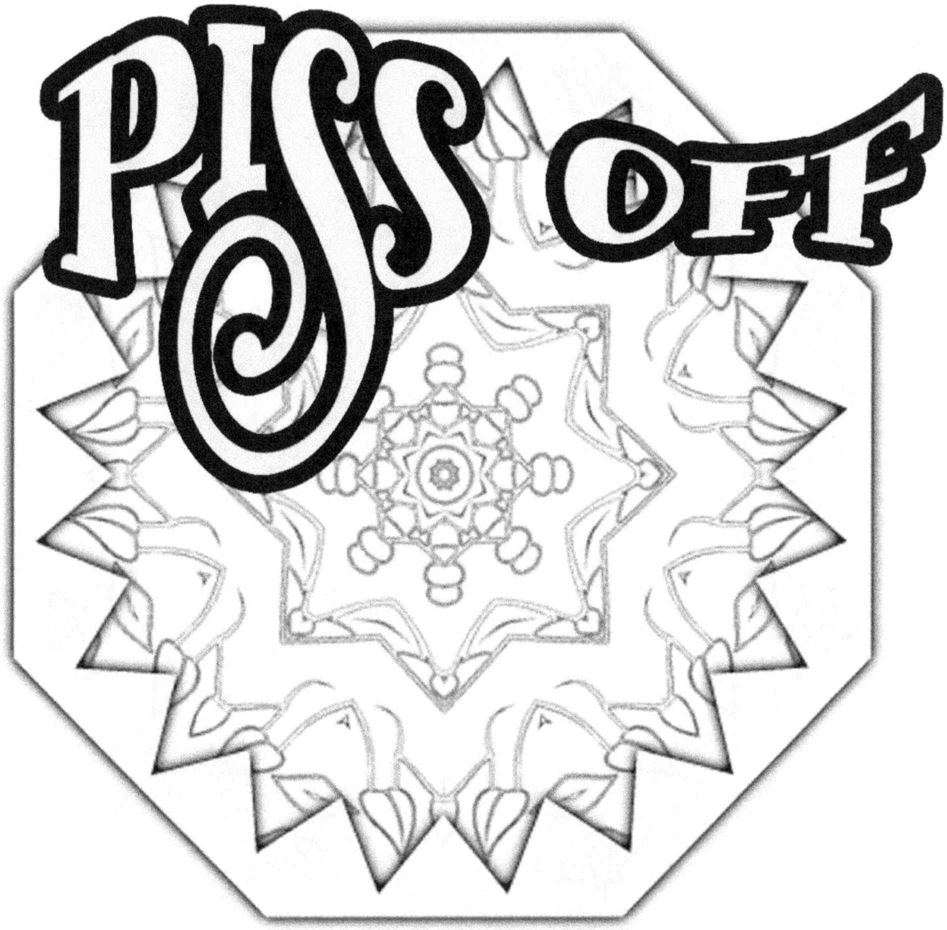
PISS OFF

Note

www.ingramcontent.com/pod-product-compliance
Lightning Source LLC
Chambersburg PA
CBHW080638190526
45169CB00009B/3424
* 9 7 8 1 5 3 3 0 6 4 8 4 4 *